# The Trouble
# with
# Women

# The Trouble with Women

by
**Diana Bahtishi**

ISBN: 1-55517-495-7

Published by Bonneville Books

Distributed by:

925 North Main, Springville, UT 84663 • 801/489-4084

CFI Publishing and Distribution Since 1986

Cedar Fort, Incorporated

CFI Distribution • CFI Books • Council Press • Bonneville Books

Typeset by Virginia Reeder
Cover design by Adam Ford
Cover design © 2000 by Lyle Mortimer

Printed in the United States of America

# Acknowledgment

A special thanks to my husband for all his support and his ability to laugh along with me. And to my children for allowing me the time to write, in between pouring Kool-aide and answering the door.

# Dedication

For women everywhere—I hope it makes you smile.

# Prologue

"What's the trouble with women?" This question has been on the tongue of every man since the dawn of time.

I will attempt to unlock the mysteries of our great gender using this book as the key to what the trouble with women is, as it covers the many facets of our lives. We will explore together different aspects of being a woman that we had no idea were trouble. Are you ready to embark on a journey? A journey through space and time.... Okay I'm done playing host of the Twilight Zone. It's really a lot simpler than this. It's just that my husband, an engineer, said I needed an introduction.

Being a woman I've laughed along with my friends for years about various aspects of being a woman. I've decided that sometimes if we could just sit down and take a good hard introspective look at ourselves, we would be laughing. It's good not to take yourself too seriously. I enjoy having a good laugh at men as well, because what I find the most interesting is how we interact together. Which can lead to some very confusing situations. So here's my version of *The Trouble With Women*.

# Chapter 1

# The Trouble:
# Is All In The Mind

The number one enemy facing women today is our conscience. Putting it simply...guilt. We feel guilty for not spending enough time with our children (even if they're teenagers and don't want us around) or at work (doesn't matter that we're employee of the month.) We feel guilty for burning dinner (so what microwave popcorn can burn), for yelling at the dog (he's an emotional puppy), for leaving the TV on (we're not conserving energy), for forgetting to do everyone's laundry (after all, our husband doesn't have two hands), for speeding (we were in labor), for the civil war (our ancestors were there), and basically for all the problems involving anyone we ever come in contact with. You think I'm exaggerating? Just listen next time your friend calls you on the phone. What is she worried about? The fact that she said something that might have offended somebody else, who she just met and will probably never meet again.

Perhaps she sent her kid to his room for burning down the woods and needs to know if the punishment is too severe. If we don't assure her that she's not a "bad mother," she will carry the guilt around until the little pyromaniac grows up and becomes an arsonist; then she will blame herself, saying, "It is all because he was scarred as a child from spending to much time in his room."

Guilt—what an amazing thing! Now I am assuming that God put guilt here for a reason. Like if we found somebody's wallet, we would return it. But you see, God made guilt before he made woman. Since man was already here needing something to do, God figured that when woman went overboard with guilt it would be man's job to tell her how irrational she was behaving. But there is a problem: we never believe men, or more commonly, they are the cause of our guilt.

Men will wait for the perfect time to spring guilt upon us. Just as we pull a beautiful seven-layer cake out of the oven (for their birthday) they will say, "Did you get any laundry done?" which of course we didn't because we spent all day baking the seven-layer cake.

And when they offer to help with the laundry this just makes us feel incompetent and our guilt begins to sky rocket! So what do we do? We eat half of the seven layer cake! Turning our guilt into nausea.

### Children

So, God decided to give us children to make up for the lousy job men were doing relieving our guilt. However, this only offered our guilt more avenues.

Now we have to feel guilty for switching laundry detergents. Is it affecting the comfortableness of our children's pj's? It doesn't matter that we can hear them snoring all the way down the hall. Are the greasy fries we served them going to someday be the reason they have an aneurysm? When we read sixteen books to them at bedtime, and they want more, will it affect their reading level if we stop now? Supreme guilt—we ate the last freezer pop!

Children have a built-in radar that detects guilt-sensitive people, namely mothers and grandmothers. When we promised them two days before that on Wednesday we would take them on a picnic, then on Wednesday we wake up with a headache and covered in hives (probably from the last picnic), we tell them we'll do it another time. So, what do they do? They put on a sad face (that could win an Oscar) and whine, "Buuut you prooomised." Suddenly, we find ourselves dragging our pockmarked body out of bed, packing a bottle of Caladryl and loading the car with a picnic basket.

Children are the masters when it comes to producing guilt. My children had been fighting continuously for almost ... well ... most their lives when I finally told them it had to stop.

I said, "The next time you get angry go to your room instead of sumo wrestling on the living room floor."

Of course, "Lecture Number 99" only lasted through the night as they slept. The next morning the buzzer went off and they took their corners for round

3

two. I, of course, tired of being awakened this way, (and being the sweet, sunny person I am in the morning), yelled at them and sent them to their rooms.

When they quieted down, I went to talk to my seven-year-old son about using his sister for a punching bag.

He listened to what I said, then, overlooking his recent attack on his sister, said, "We're supposed to go to our rooms when we're angry."

"That's right, so why didn't you?" I replied.

I didn't realize until later he meant me. Guilt can wait if it's not convenient.

## Mothers

Better than husbands and children at guilt production are our own mothers. Our own mothers are so good at it they can do it without even making a face.

"So how are my grandchildren doing in school? Better I hope."

We reply, "Fine," and then sit and twist on this all day long, saying to ourselves, "What did she mean by that? I am doing the best I can. She doesn't know what it's like to raise four kids and hold a job." We will list all the things we are sure our mother could never have experienced raising us.

If she doesn't try the "children" guilt department of our brain, our mother will try others.

"Is that what you're wearing to dinner?" she'll

ask. Then she'll watch us play with our dress all night.

Now fed up, we will say something to make her feel guilty. We watch, anticipating a reaction, only to observe her smiling sweetly with love in her eyes. Then we end up going to bed feeling even more guilty. Thinking, "How could I say that to mom? The woman who gave me life and my first guilt trip?"

Well, if you're looking to me, the most guilt-stricken woman to walk the face of the earth, whose mother's name is in the dictionary under "guilt transmitter," to solve this great trouble of ours, my answer would be...good luck. I only state the problems, I don't find the solutions. I am just a writer, not Ghandi. Oh! Now I am feeling guilty for having let you down. Maybe I led you on. All right, how about we all say in sync, "I am never going to feel guilty again." Hum a little. Come on...you're not sharing! Well, it's not working, I still feel guilty. You're not giving enough of yourself. All right, I won't make you feel guiltier. That won't solve anyone's problems, although it might lessen some of mine. Maybe I could load a few of my other problems on the reader as well.

Okay. I know you didn't pay money to feel guilty. So, we as women are just going to have to stop feeling guilty! We will no longer feel guilty when our children do their spiel about how we didn't breastfeed them or when our husbands ask us where all the money went.

We will no longer feel guilty when our mothers ask how much we weigh. We will no longer feel guilty for the problems in the world, saying, "If I had only saved that soda can I could have recycled it, made a new wheel for my son's bike out of it, and sent the nickel to Israel to feed a family of four on 'just pennies a day.'"

I myself am sick and tired of feeling guilty for everything and make a pledge with my sisters that I will no longer feel guilty. It will stop right now! This very instant! It will never enter my mind again. I will just live my life being a good mom completely guilt-free. There, I feel better, and if I really think I can do this for more than fifteen seconds, I've got more problems than guilt to worry about.

## Chapter 2

## The Trouble:
## Got To Get A Deal

What is this force that drives us twenty miles out of our way to find a T-shirt marked a dollar off? Could it be the fact that when we find one, it feels like we just won the lottery? "Wow! I saved a dollar! With the money I saved buying this T-shirt, in fifty years, I can go to Disneyland!"

Crazy as it seems, we as women love to get a deal. Even those of us who can afford not to. It's part of our nature to look for a deal. Haven't you ever heard ladies snickering in the dressing room, "Ha! Hah! I got a deal and I didn't even have to."

### Expeditions for deals

Women will look anywhere for a bargain. When looking for bargains we suddenly become Indiana Jones, risking our very lives for that precious knick-knack. Knocking on doors of big hairy men covered in tattoos, we'll say, "I'm here about those tea cups you had advertised in the paper. Where? Oh? Down in the basement? Oh, sure, I'll come down and look." Traveling to foreign countries, saying, "Do you speak English? I want to buy the pottery! No, without the snake!"

And we love to drag our friends on these adventures in the outback. Our husbands won't come along—they learned their lesson the first time. "Oh come on, Jack, those gangs over there are just misunderstood boyz-in-the-hood. They need those weapons to defend themselves from the police. See, they're waving. Now see that shack that they are standing in front of? That's where we are going to get the Corningware."

### Yard sales

We also love to think we are making a deal even when we aren't. That's why we have yard sales. We spend weeks going through all the junk in our house, collecting it into one big area. We arrange it ever so orderly on tables in the yard so people can rearrange it. We willingly let strangers into our home to see some old chair so they can eye our valuables and decide when's the best time to rob us. Then we sell it for like...a nickel. And when it's all over and we've made twenty bucks, we buy it all back the next weekend at someone else's yard sale. Yes, we are "wheelers and dealers."

Now, let's think about what is going on here. Let's think about this "rationally" (don't you hate that word?). Someone is selling "stuff" out in their yard. They no longer want this "stuff" in their house. They used the "stuff" for forty years, and it shows. They think perhaps someone will treasure their dog's blanket. And we will! It's a nickel! What a deal! It doesn't matter what it is, the cheapest thing always gets sold! Men are smarter: they only do this if it's a car part, saying, "I might need this. If I ever get a porsche."

My friend has a nice word for yard sales. She calls them "garbage sales." Of course this didn't stop her from buying every weekend, but at least she was honest about what she was getting.

## Trinket shopping

A lot of my friends love to trinket shop. Not the diamond kind but the kind you possess fifty of and have to dust every thirty minutes.

The sit-on-your-shelf-and-collect-dust collections are priceless to women. If one gets broken, it ruins the whole collection, driving us so insane that we have to run down to the dollar store and buy another one. As we fight traffic, sweating and panicking all the way, saying, "What if they're sold out?" We can't rest until we replace it. Heaven forbid this should happen after store hours.

## Shop-a-holics

Well, much to the shame of the bargain hunters there are those who deviate from the righteous path.

Yes, not all women just bargain shop. Some just shop all the time.

Regardless of the cost, they buy every little knick-knack they see, much to the mental duress of their husbands. Doesn't matter if they aren't even sure what the items are. They will say, "It was just so cute I had to have it. No, I don't know what it does or what it's purpose is. Does it have to have one?" Watching them explain this to their husbands is even more entertaining. "Yes it has a name. It's a "Klikkimister." It's for klikking. Well on the infomercial, it was something like this, but if you're going to get technical, (which men will) just never mind!" That's how we get out of everything.

When these women have children, the buying gets even more out of control. Not only do these women have to have everything, but for their children as well. "Doesn't Junior look cute in his bonnet." they say as junior chews the strings to ribbons. These around the clock shoppers usually have the most yard sales with lots of "Klikkmisters" for sale.

## Coupons

Aren't coupons a wonderful thing! I have a friend who can buy eighty dollars worth of food, whip out her coupons and pay thirty cents. When I try to save coupons, they end up in a big pile behind the refrigerator, and when I find them, they have expired. By then I'm too tired for shopping anyway. So I guess they are saving me money. But it never fails that I am always behind the woman in the checkout line with 50 coupons, who needs a price check on yogurt, because she said it was 10 cents overpriced. I once overheard a customer offer to pay a woman the twenty-five cent difference just to keep the line moving. People are so charitable at Christmas.

## Blue light specials

Aren't these a waste of time! They should call these black and blue specials because after we have finished fighting with fifty women over a sleeveless blouse, we need the sleeves to cover our bruises.

We seem to panic when we see the blue light flashing. It must have something to do with getting pulled over by the police, except this time we want the ticket. That light goes on and you can feel the store lean to one side as everyone rushes towards the light. I think the light must hold some kind of "hypnotic beam" developed by store owners to get rid of all their "the-hems-gonna-come-out-before-you-get-home-with-it" specials. Apparently, bluelight specials are not just an earthly event because women always tell you that when it's your time to die, "Go towards the light."

## Size it up

Another factor involved in these specials is the "one-size-fits-all" theory. Whoever coined this phrase was a man. Yeah, one size fits all if you don't breathe, and want to look stupid. It's just like the small, medium, and large theory. Now let's say you're a 400 pound woman but you consider yourself small-boned, thus assuming you could fit in a medium right? Only if it's spandex.

This is amazing material. The one material that can fit anybody and it's amazing how many people take advantage of that.

You see, we as women, in order to be in fashion, will wear anything regardless of how ridiculous it looks on us. If car parts suddenly came into fashion, how many of us would be up late while our husband's slept, trying on the seatcovers of his new convertible? I have tried on skirts I couldn't walk in, saying to my friend, "Maybe you could just wheel me into the party." When we finally buy this skirt it is only because we kept it on too long in the dressing room, and it cut off the oxygen to our brain.

How many of us have excitingly gone shopping the minute after giving birth, thinking, "The baby's been born, everything's back to normal." Yeah, as normal as it will ever be.

## Catalog shopping

"Welcome to Fantasy Island." The clothes adorning the girls in these pictures are on girls who had a pickle and lettuce for lunch, not three leftover Happy Meals and pie. But we order from it anyway. Then we blame the manufacturer when we don't look like the twelve-year-old girl in the picture, saying, "They messed up my order. I'm a size eight, and this can't be a size eight. I don't even think it's the same outfit."

And of course when we order an item with a defect because we "got a deal," we are surprised when we have to return it. Well, I don't know about you, ladies, but I don't have a lot of use for four-legged pantyhose.

The truth is, it's just in our genes to shop for a deal. Buying useless items off blue light specials. We might as well enjoy ourselves doing it. After all, it's tradition.

## Chapter 3

## The Trouble:
## Got To Feel Pretty

"How do I look?" We always ask this question; especially before we go out. Men don't ask us this! Men don't care! They just reply, "Fine, get in the car."

Why do we say this? Do we expect men to fall at our feet and say, "I have never seen such an enchanting beauty"? Instead we get "Fine, get in the car." I think the reason we bother to ask this is because after childbirth we want to know if we still have "it" or at least what end of our body "it" went to.

Everywhere we turn, we are bombarded by pictures of glamorous women. Women whose only experience with childbirth was their own. As we wait in line at the grocery store, we watch the teenage boy ahead of us ogle the pictures of models on the cover of magazines. Then, as he turns and sees us with our children and the deep stress lines they've put in our face, he cringes in horror as if we're some yet-unevolved species of the food chain.

That alone is why we try so hard to look attractive. We are trying to keep pace with the thirty-five-year-old actress in the picture who is really airbrushed. So we buy the matching outfit with the matching earrings and the matching hat and shoes. Why? So we can look like "Dolly Dress up"? We spend hours getting our hair done. Buying the gels and spritz and sprays. Knowing at any moment someone could light up a cigarette near us and it would all be over. We buy the crimpers, the curling irons, the hot rollers, the gentle rollers, the roller coasters. We must have body to our dried out, frizzed out, chemically treated hair.

We buy the makeup to paint some beauty or color on, because there are so many colors. Colors I didn't even know existed, like "Mellow Pink," "Splashy Red" and "Jaded Green." We believe these colors, that are nonexistent in the real world, are going to look good on us. What is "Splashy Red?"

If we can get through choosing the colors, putting them on is an even harder trick. Have you ever looked at the black and white diagram on the back of the eyeshadow box and been able to figure out which shade to put where? How are we supposed to blend these rainbow colors into one so we will look...natural? I don't think it's possible. As far as I know, the only babies born with orange-green eyelids had a bad case of jaundice. And I don't think that's the look we're going for.

## Lip lining

Boy, this is risky! Every time I do this, I worry someone's going to yell, "Hey Bozo, the circus starts in five minutes!" My lips always come out the shape of two strategically placed bananas. One is always crooked, making me appear like I spent my day at the dentist.

## Blushing

I never know how to aim the blush. I know I'm supposed to bring my cheekbones out. I just don't know which direction.

## Eyebrows

If you want to live dangerously, eyebrows are a lot of fun. There are many looks you can create with these things. There's the "You-just-scared-the-daylights-out-of-me" look.

The "What's-that-crawling-across-your-fore-head" look. If you keep getting smacked in the head with newspapers...you're wearing this look. The "clown-for-hire" look or the "Silent-screen-star" look of desperation and misery. I hate having mine done. I tend to wait until they are growing out of my ears. Once, to save time, I had mine plucked and dyed at the same time. Do you know that dye burns when it enters an open wound and that you go home with the "Puffy-Frankenstein" look? After your husband laughs at your attractive new look for a couple of hours, the salon attendant calls and warns you to go to the hospital if it gets worse.

My friend once decided to do hers with a home hot wax treatment. She ripped them off her face.

## Getting the skinny

You'd think doing all of these beauty procedures would be time-consuming enough, but don't forget the time we spend on our lifelong quest, "to be thinner than our best friends." So we get up in the morning, eat some Special K; by the time we're done packing our kids' lunches we've eaten half a bologna sandwich, some chips, and licked the frosting off their cake. And we don't understand why that cereal isn't keeping us trim.

We seem to expect that by just eating the cereal, the pounds should drop off. If it doesn't work, we buy some magic pill with a tough name like "fat killer" or "fat serial killer." It usually just gives us heartburn. So then we try alternative treatments like watching aerobics and infomercials on fat reduction, in hopes that the waves from the TV will combine with our brain waves and we will lose weight. A mind is a powerful thing. It's also a "terrible thing to waste."

My best friend in high school dropped excess pounds by eating Hershey bars for breakfast. It didn't help her self-esteem though, because everywhere we went she would say, "Is my butt as big as hers?" She looked great, but she now had the "I can be thinner, stronger, better than her" complex. I call it the "Bionic woman syndrome." Wouldn't we all love to be Jamie Summers.

### Exercise

I really hate to exercise, but I do it, and I'll tell you why. It's plain and simple—I've had four children. I've got to put things back where they used to be. It is not gravity that moves these parts around, it's suction. Women who have pushed out things the size of watermelons will understand what I'm talking about. When it's time for babies to be born they won't, because something inside their little head says, "This is going to hurt." So getting them out is like popping a cork from a bottle.

Between pregnancies I exercise. During pregnancy I exercise the right to eat. When I was pregnant I felt I didn't have to worry about being pretty. After all, you're supposed to glow, right? I had more serious concerns, like how to get out of the couch or how cherries tasted on pizza.

### Just a little bit of respect

You see women associate attractiveness with respect. Respect not just from the opposite sex but from each other. My husband will ask, "Why are you so dressed up to go to the store?" My reply, "Because I want to hand my coupons over with dignity." Men don't believe this. But I've tried it both ways. I've rushed to the store, hair hanging down in my face, no makeup, and my check had to be approved twice. Then I fixed myself up and wrote that baby for twenty dollars over.

Upon entering a doctor's office as a pregnant woman wearing sweats, the receptionist asked, "You're pregnant again?" In designer maternity attire, she asked, "When's your baby due?"

## Obsession

Anyhow, this obsession with being pretty is really a waste of time. It's okay to be attractive and look the best we can, but look at all the time we could save if we just shaved and ran out the door like men. After all, what do men say after they marry us? "I married you for what's on the inside not the outside...so get in the car."

# Chapter 4

# The Trouble:
# Becoming Our Mothers

Being like are mothers is inevitable. It happens whether we want it to or not. When I was growing up my mom thought I was crazy because I didn't love polyester. Instead I loved jeans, rock n' roll, wild hair and anything else she had picketed against in her youth.

I didn't know what I wanted to be but it wasn't a ballerina, a piano player, a tap dancer, a swimmer, or one of the many other lessons she enrolled me in trying to help me reach my fullest potential or at least something. She didn't know what to make of me. So she coined the phrase, "You're just like your father."

The day after my last child was born, I found myself in polyester, wearing no makeup and sporting a ponytail. What are the first words out of her mouth when she comes to visit, "I don't like your hair that way. You're just like your father." I replied, "Mom, look at me! You've won...I'm you!"

## Secret disease

This disease we harbor, to be like our mothers, is not something we discuss with our friends. We wouldn't dare admit this to our friends since we spend so much time laughing at our mothers with them. Face it, there are no normal parents (childbirth does something to your mind). We may think we are nowhere as weird as our parents but look at some of the weird things we repeat to our kids.

For example:

1. "You do that again and your face will get stuck like that."

Now have we ever in our lives seen anyone walking around with their eyelids flipped up, saying, "I did it again. My mom warned me but I was only six."

2. "Eat your eggs or you'll have slow children."

This was my mom's favorite; however, the eggs didn't help.

3. "Your father and I always played by ourselves."

Huh, that explains it.

4. "When I was your age I had the same problem."

Isn't this a comfort for our child? To know that

life is a vicious cycle doomed to repeat itself? How do we remember what our problems were when we were four anyway?

5. "When you're eighteen you'll be ready to move out on your own."

Huh, try thirteen.

6. "What was going through your mind!"

Do we really want to know the answer to this?

## The transformation

We seem to transform into our mother overnight. If this was a gradual thing maybe we could stop it. Instead, we wake up one morning, wearing curlers and support hose, look in the mirror and say, "I've become my mother!" When I start sounding like my mother my husband will laugh and say, "You've become your mother," and I'll say, "Yeah and you, your father" and the laughter stops.

I have a great mom except for one thing. She is the most considerate person on the face of the earth. She will sacrifice at every opportunity. For example, she'll say, "I need to use the shower, but I'll wait."

And I'll reply, "But mom, it's your house."

She will say, "I want to come visit if it's not a bad time."

"But mom, it's always a bad time when you're here," I tease. I am surprised she eats our food and uses our towels when she visits. She doesn't want to be a bother. She even brings her own sheets. I tell her we have sheets. "Oh, I like mine," she says. What's the difference—a sheet is a sheet, right? She brings her own soap and toilet paper, sometimes, even her favorite piece of furniture. Sometimes I wonder: is she coming to visit or slowly moving in? She seems to be bringing everything from the attic and the basement of her house. She says she is trying to get rid of it before she dies, but what makes her think I want it? It will just go in my basement and I'll just have to get rid of it before I die. Maybe she is starting a tradition? I wish she'd just leave memories.

## My mom is Dear Abbey

My mom loves to give advice, which always starts out with "I don't want to hurt your feelings, but..." The advice seems to get stranger by the year. She once told me that the reason my oldest daughter teased boys was because I let her watch "The Little Mermaid" too many times. I replied, "Shhh, someone will hear you and lock you up."

And the excuses she comes up with for my children are astounding. She once rationalized that the reason my daughter was pummeling her brother was because she had eaten one too many Coco Puffs. As with all drugs those things are pretty potent.

## Multi-talented mom

Besides her advice-giving my mom has many other talents. She is wonderful at sewing and is absolutely positive I can do the same. She confidently hands me a pre-cut pattern (she thinks that will help), saying, "Here, you can just whip this up tonight." Of course, I can't use the machine without sewing my fingers together. She doesn't know I already asked my husband if he thought it was too late to get a refund on it.

My mom also loves to garden. She wonders why I don't share her enthusiasm; she forgets she used to wake me up at 5:00 a. m. to pull weeds. Yes, that increased my love of the field. She can grow anything, while I have to buy imitation house plants. If anything survives two weeks in my house we name it and raise a plaque to it.

## Mom the worrier

My mother really cares about people. But she worries about everything. She worried about one of my children's crooked toes, telling me that we could construct a splint out of popsicle sticks. If he wore it on his toes at night it would correct the toe problem. I said, "Mom, he's beautiful, who is going to look at his toes?"

She regrets ever giving me braces, saying, "I should have just had you hold your buck teeth in with your finger while you watched TV." When I laugh she says, "They weren't that buck," and I laugh harder.

These weird mother ideas must be the effects of all the hormones racing through our body during pregnancy. Of course, my hormones were trained after delivering three kids in six years; they never bothered to change back to normal, they just went in their corners to wait.

## Stands out in a crowd

Mom, as crazy as she seems, is still allowed to wander around loose. I think because she is one of those oddities of nature that causes people to stare in awe. On the street she even stops teen girls who are puffing on cigarettes, and tells them that smoking will give them flabby breasts.

Mom is used to being teased about her quirkiness and has a good sense of humor about it. In fact, I share some of her sense of humor. She once baked a loaf of bread that was so hard my father took it and placed it behind the back tire of the car to keep it from rolling down hill. Okay, maybe I share more of my father's sense of humor. Maybe I am "just like my father."

However, my mother has always been able to laugh at herself after falling—or maybe that's while watching me fall. So I suppose we share some similar qualities because I can laugh at her falling too.

## Never to be our mother

Listing our mothers' talents can make us depressed, thinking we suffer in comparison. Then our husband comes home and we cry, saying, "I'll never be my mother." And he smiles in relief and says, "Thank goodness!"

# Chapter 5

# The Trouble:
# M&M's

I've heard men joke about the emotional states of women. Well, they would be a nervous wreck too if their body behaved like a three ring circus. Something is constantly going on in one area or another of our bodies and there is nothing we can do about it.

Men only have two crisis in life, puberty and forty. We have the "four M's": Maturity , Menstruation, Maternity and Menopause. We never get a break. I would welcome just a mid-life crisis.

## Maturity

Maturity is the first little crisis. Everything is blossoming and growing to make us look like our mother before she had us. We can no longer fit into anything we wore the week before. Everything is either too short, too tight or too babyish for our coming of age.

## Menstruation

After maturity, menstruation comes every month to remind us that we are a woman now. The first time we have a good cry with our mothers, for the next forty years we cry by ourselves, because of that PMS (Pretty Mean Spirited) stuff, which was given to naive women to encourage them to get pregnant, not realizing it was only worse. So if we think about it, two weeks are spent each month out of our lives being irrational, cranky and moody (and we wonder why men like fishing). As if that's not enough, we gain about two hundred pounds of water and have bouts of hysteria. And no matter what our husbands do, it hurts our feelings. "Why did you buy me a soda? If I retain any more water, I'll be a Jacuzzi. Where are you going with the kids; are you trying to escape?"

## Maternity

The next "M" is maternity. This one is nine full months of turmoil plus postpartum depression. Yippie! My husband claims this is when he noticed his first gray hair.

Pregnancy starts out with nausea that compares to being E. coli poisoned. I once threw up out the window of a car going fifty-five mph, much to the astonishment of the people in the passing lane.

By the ninth month everything is swollen, including our husband's arm where we've punched him for the last seven. We have stretch marks that look like we've been wrestling lions and we find the weight is not "all baby" but has been evenly distributed all over our body. And if that's not bad enough, we usually end up going to some male doctor who tells us we're gaining too much weight, as we stare at his gut, thinking, "Well at least mine doesn't shake like a 'bowl full of jelly.'"

Now, I have encountered some women who love every minute of pregnancy. Frankly, I think these women are suffering from some hormone deficiency. I even had one tell me that labor was a "rush" for her. Mine was a rush too—to get the baby out.

Women who want to have natural childbirth always amaze me. I say, "Why go natural when God gave us drugs?" I once told a doctor I wanted an epidural and the nurse overheard and said, "Yeah, you can just hook her up the eighth month." I would have liked that. This doctor did get me an epidural. After the delivery, a nurse entered the room and asked about my condition. Unable to feel anything from the waist down, I replied, "Can't feel my legs, might have to go to the bathroom, but hey, who cares!"

The third child was completely natural and the nurse had to leave the room during delivery to keep from laughing because I kept screaming, "Can't you just pull it out! Just get down in there and pull!"

The first child was quite stressful on my husband, who had to lean on my shoulder quite a bit because he didn't feel well. I know. Can you believe it? It was bad enough that he dropped me along with my luggage on the steps of the hospital in a wet dress (my water had broken) so that I could be publicly humiliated while he parked. We also made the mistake of telling everyone we were on our way to the hospital. People were phoning me all through the delivery. That never happened again because the next time I never told anyone I was pregnant.

If pregnancy has taught me one thing, it's that for some reason, once you're pregnant, your body is open for viewing. Everybody has seen it at least twice on the maternity ward and all we can hope for is that they liked what they saw.

There is a beauty to pregnancy and that is the only reason we do it. To annoy our husbands for nine months.

## Menopause

Now menopause. I have only heard the horror stories on this one. I think God gave us menopause to make us thankful for menstruation and maternity. I've heard women complain menopause makes them forgetful, but that's nothing new—I do that pregnant. I once told a lady a story and two seconds later I forgot I told her the story and started to repeat it again. In the middle of it, I said, "...and I just told you this, didn't I? It's the pregnancy, I promise I'm really not like this." I don't think she bought it. I'm blonde, you know. Anyhow, a friend of mine is going through menopause and she can't remember anything. Of course, I think she was like that before. I don't remember.

Actually, there is a lot to look forward to when our child-bearing years are over. I have plans to fill my grandchildren with candy, spin them around and put them in their parents' car for the long journey home.

Although we go through a lot of changes, being a woman is a great thing; after all, we can bring life into the world. Also, in this day and age, we have epidurals to make it easier to bring in life.

## Chapter 6

## The Trouble:
## Our Hearts Are Mushy


Women have the gene that cries at Hallmark commercials. We see sweet old grandma receiving a card from her granddaughter (who hasn't visited her in ten years) and we say, "Oh that's beautiful," then start to cry. While men are saying, "If she were a better granddaughter she would be visiting her on her birthday. The card is the cheap way out." I sense they are not feeling what we are.

I have a friend who can see any touching commercial and cry. She watches a lot of TV alone. It's amazing the things that make us cry. If we see a commercial about a woman with dishpan hands, whose dream is to have a dishwasher, we will cry when she gets one.

I hate this aspect of being a woman because my husband is more interested to see if I am crying than watching the movie. So he can tease, "Oh, are you crying?" I've decided this is one of men's little tricks.

They figure if they make fun of us instead of watching the movie they won't start crying. However, I've gotten tougher. I don't cry at everything. I won't give my husband the satisfaction.

## Weddings

Now I don't understand why we cry at these functions. I could understand if we were the father of the bride and have to pay for it. However if we are the mother of the son who we've been cooking and cleaning up after the past twenty years and he finally found some poor sucker to take over for the next fifty, we should be happy!

My mother said she almost cried at my wedding. I thought, "And what you remembered you were getting rid of me?" How do you think the couple getting married feels when they turn around to see everyone sobbing? Do you think this gives them hope for their future? They are probably wondering if the old married couples know something they don't? At my wedding, I was too nervous to cry. I was shaking so badly I could barely hold the bouquet. Much the opposite of my husband, who was in the next room playing cards up to two minutes before he walked down the aisle. He may not have understood then, but for what it's worth, fourteen years and four kids later, he's crying now.

## Baby showers

Baby showers are another event that make women cry. We just look at that precious baby and remember how much delivering our own hurt. I think that's pretty cut-and-dried, don't you?

## People who take advantage: children

The people best at taking advantage of our soft hearts are children. You see, children know our soft hearts make it harder for us to say "no" because we want them to be happy. This enables them to be able to wear us down faster. This was the first rule my children learned in life: "Mommies will break, we just have to use the right tactic to do it." They have also learned that mom gets over her anger quickly, so they figure, "If we wait until she calms down we can ask her again." My daughter can walk in the house, pass her father in the living room calmly, and as soon as she enters my room turn into a hysterical, tear-flooding maniac, telling me some great trauma she just experienced outside. Once I asked her if she passed her father on her way in; she calmly replied, "Yeah, I said hi."

Children always come to mom to whine. Do they think this is a foreign language that only their mother can decipher? "She hit me with the baaaaalll in the llllleggggg."

My four year old just comes to me and says, "Spank her! She needs a spanking." She is very direct. Mothers will tolerate their children longer then anyone.

We to them are a Duracell battery.

## Friends

We are also sympathetic to our friends who call us with stories that sound like they have been watching Jerry Springer.

Yet our husbands, when listening to their friends' sob stories, can just slap them on the back and say, "Well, don't die on me, Dan." I guess this meets a man's requirement for sympathy.

Although they tease us, I think men are grateful we like to cry so much and are so forgiving. After all, didn't they tell us they love us for our kindness, and the fact we don't have to pretend we have something in our eye.

## Justifications for soft hearts

God gave us soft hearts so we would feed the poor, clothe the needy, and change diapers. He knew we would need these hearts to heal the world and let our husbands win at Monopoly. He knew we would need them to love babies, nurture children and refrain from swearing when debating the price with grocery clerks.

However, some women do need to get a grip. Like the ones we see on TV who are crying and bellowing, "My husband is addicted to Alpo and left me for the dog, but I still love him. Please come back." All right, this is taking it too far. It's not her heart that's soft, it's her head. These kind of women make the rest of us look bad. Misinformed men get the idea that we will put up with anything (men who have obviously never been around a pregnant woman).

### Soft but tough

We are soft but we can be pushed too far. All we ask is to be treated with respect, and if we aren't, our motto should be "Boy! You gonna find out what soft is by the lump on your head!"

Finding a good man can be tough. Sometimes we think, "Oh, he'll change." But let me tell you, sister, if he says he'd like to kill people, all the softness and sweetness isn't going to change a thing. Keep the softness below your neck.

# Chapter 7

# The Trouble:
# We're Over Analyzers Supreme

Women are wonderful analyzers. We seem to be able to make something out of practically nothing every single time. If we could market this skill we would be very rich. However, if we ever stopped and listened to ourselves, we would realize how ludicrous we really sound. But who has time to listen when you're busy analyzing?

## Analyzing friends

We're always analyzing our friends, saying, "Well, I think her problem lies deep within herself. She just doesn't respect herself enough."

And our husbands reply, "Honey, she shot her husband."

"Yes, yes, I know, but you see, if she respected herself she wouldn't be going to prison." As our husbands stand there looking confused. We add, "Yes, that's how I see it. She didn't really mean to kill him, just inflict pain."

"Honey, she shot him in the head at close range!"

We also analyze what we say. "I wonder what she meant by that?"

Husbands say, "Honey, she said you look nice."

We reply, "No, she said 'Gee, you look nice.' Like she was surprised I could look nice."

"That's not what she meant!"

"Oh sure, take her side. How can you draw that conclusion? I know her and you don't. She can be very vicious."

They say, "But she said you look nice!"


## Children

We analyze our children. "He's not really happy."

Our husband says, "He looks happy. He has stopped crying and is playing in the sandbox."

"His knee still hurts him."

"How can you tell?" husbands ask.

"Look at it, doesn't it look like it hurts! If you fell and skinned your knee it would hurt, right?"

"Yes," our husbands reply.

"Well, there you go, he's not happy." Analyzing

our children usually leads us to panic or hysteria.

"She says her tummy hurts," we say.

"It's probably just gas," they reply.

"Do you have to go to the bathroom?"

"No, Mommy."

"It's not gas." We say

"Where does it hurt, honey?"

"Right here, Daddy."

"She probably has the flu," they say.

"No, I think she has an acute appendicitis," we say.

"What? Honey, if she had an acute appendicitis she would be howling and screaming and we would know. She probably just ate too many popsicles."

"All right, just remember it's on your head if anything happens to my baby. I tried to suggest the possibilities," we say.

"I'll call the ambulance," our husband says in despair.

## Husbands

We also analyze our husbands. "So what are you thinking?" we ask.

"Nothing."

"You must be thinking something, you're not saying anything," we reply.

"Nothing, I'm just reading the paper," they reply.

"So you don't want to talk to me—is that why you're reading the paper?"

"No, I just want to know what is happening in the world."

"Oh, and I don't," we reply.

"Honey, I just want to read the paper!"

"All right, read your stupid paper—I know what you're really doing!"

The problem with analyzing is that we are sure we know all the answers.

## My mother the analyzer

My mother is wonderful at analyzing. According to her, my kids never do anything wrong; my mom will say, "It's their vitamin deficiency that makes them fight." I watch her in amazement because when I was little and in trouble the only excuses I ever heard came from me when I saw her coming. And vitamin deficiency never entered her head.

If my dad ever said anything about somebody else my mom would make some weird excuse for them saying, "Well, they are probably just busy or they would have called; I think he has mental problems."

Dad would answer, "So does that mean if you're busy with mental problems you can't drop by?" Of course, my dad is rational. He learned to just agree with my mom and say "Yep, he's a dummy all right. He's a head short of owning a brain."

It's hard to try and stop analyzing. Especially with my children. Sometimes, I just say, "Well, if you don't feel well, lie down! If you think you're going to die, call me. I'd like to be there for that." Analyzing can make us really tired. I usually have to lie down after talking with my twelve year old.

## The talent to spin

Sometimes women say or do things just to spin each other up. This is done by answering a simple question in a matter-of-fact way.

"So did you like those cookies?"

"Yeah."

"Were they good?"

"Yeah."

"Did you like them?"

"Yesss!"

"Well, you are quiet!"

"I'm reading the paper."

## Spinning men

It's not easy for us to spin men up because if we give them a leading answer they don't care. Then we are the ones who get spun up and say, "Didn't you just hear the way I answered you?"

They reply, "You said 'fine.'"

"Well, I didn't mean it!"

"Well, you said it! So, if you say it, you mean it!"

Poor men, they are under the impression if we say something we mean it. They haven't learned the skill of reading between the lines yet. We must give them a lot of grief. My husband once said he thought the reason God gave us families is because he figured if we could survive them we could survive anything. I think he was serious. If I am analyzing correctly.

My son has the male view. He just takes you on your word. When he was six, I had to change the baby in a public restroom. I rushed all my children into the ladies' room. My son stared curiously at the different appliances on the walls. In particular, he stared at the one I was laying the baby on and said, "What is that?"

"This is for changing babies," I replied (it was a changing table).

His eyes widened in his head and he said, "It makes them different!" Well, no analyzing there.

I suppose there is good and bad to both ways of thinking. The men's way looks easier and saves time, but they are not aware of people's feelings.

I will say, "I think she was upset."

"She didn't say she was," he replies.

"Honey, she discussed suicide all night."

## Rules to analyze by

There are two rules to remember when analyzing. They can mean the difference between being on the right track or working your way to the funny farm. First, is what you are thinking humanly possible? Second, do you sound like your mother? If you sound like your mother, get yourself analyzed by a professional. Now, I have to read the paper and you women can analyze it all you want. Just follow the rules.

## Chapter 8

## The Trouble:
## We Can Be Better, Stronger, and Irritate Everyone Else

We've all seen her. There seems to be a clone of her everywhere. There she is—just waiting to look better than us. We usually see her at our lowest point in life: nine months pregnant, grocery shopping. Our hair is straggled down in our face. We are wearing our husband's flannel pj top because it's the only thing left that fits (and at this point we don't care). It's 11:00 in the morning and we have not a glimmer of makeup on and are still wearing our slippers.

Our children have managed to smash the bread in the cart, open the cookies and crumble them all over their faces as they argue over who gets to sit in the seat in the front of the cart.

When here she comes "zippity-do-dahing" down the aisle, singing a show tune to her kids. We turn just in time to see her whiz by effortlessly. She stops ahead to pick up some peanut butter and there she is. Her five kids are all neatly dressed—no suckers are stuck in their hair. They are all smiling sweetly, standing by the cart waiting patiently for their mother. The fifth one, a baby, calmly sucks his thumb while reading the dictionary. Everything matches on her children—even their socks and shoes. And all the girls are adorned in matching designer dresses and their neatly curled locks are topped with bows.

The woman herself is astonishing. She is wearing the latest trendy style for ladies on the go. She looks like she just stepped out of a salon. Her hair is neatly curled and she has not a smudge of eyeliner on her face. She even smells good. All the food in her cart is organized into food groups and we have to contain ourself from ramming her cart and knocking a few of those groups out of order.

We, of course, are struggling to undo what's left of our pony tail as we walk by her and pretend our pajama shirt is hip. She, of course, can't just let us pass, but has to turn with a big smile and say, "Hello, how are you?" We smile and reply, "Just wonderful." When what we really want to say is, "How do I look? Misses Perceptive! I am nine months pregnant, wearing a man's pajama shirt and slippers! I've got stretch marks down to my ankles, which are swollen, by the way! My children have just finished their breakfast of cookies and are now debating on what item they will eat or crush next! Five minutes ago it was my toe!"

But, of course, we don't say this out of respect for her and the fact that our husbands would kill us when the kids told him what we had done. You see, she is like the great buck that hunters never kill because they are something of a mystery. I suppose if we followed her to her car we would probably hear the real story on those sweetly behaved children. She would say, "Okay I'll take you to the zoo now. Just get in the car. Then one of those sweet kids would say, "I want to sit up front!" and of course they all would. Bribery only lasts so long.

Even though we only saw a brief glance of this perfect little family, the effects will traumatize us for years. We will get up the next morning at five, clean our house, style our hair, shower and dress in something shimmery. Then make omelets for our kids' breakfast, wash the car and walk the dog. Exercise for forty minutes and learn opera. Then teach our two year old to read the paper.

By noon, we will be so exhausted we will put on wrestling for the children and collapse on the couch until 5:00 p. m., when our husband comes home to find us there, and looking around, stupidly ask, "So what did you do all day?" At which point we kill him.

I have friends that go through these rituals every day. The only time you will ever see me get up at five it will be night. I am not a morning person, nor will I ever be. After all those pregnant years it's the best time for nausea. Besides, I don't want to get up too early. Then I wouldn't be able to feel sorry for my husband when he gets up at five-thirty for work. Instead, when he complains, I would just snap, "Oh, get over it!" A friend of mine gets up early every day and puts on her face and fixes her hair. Her husband travels and is never home. I asked her, "So why do you do it if you're just going to be home all day?" She replied, "Because I'm scary without it." I asked, "Who are you going to scare, your children?" "No—the neighbors." she replied.

## Weeks of routines

Some weeks I go through routines of cleaning, trying to keep up with all the work of motherhood, and then I get tired and say, "Oh what's it all for?" Then I let everything go and find out what it's all for.

I think it's because secretly I know someday everything in my life will be perfect. My house will be perfectly clean. Clean laundry will no longer be found shaped in a volcano on my bed. I will be perfectly dressed. My kids will be perfectly clean and behaved. My meals at dinner will leave everybody hungering for the next one. My car will never be out of gas and I will always have time to enjoy life. Because I will be comatose, dreaming I have a cook, maid, nanny, and chauffeur and hey—why not—butler—you have to have a scapegoat.

## Women get upset when things aren't perfect

It's true women get upset when things aren't perfect. Which is 90 percent of the time so what can we do to make things easier? Here are a few suggestions:

1. Have our makeup tattooed on.

2. Shave our heads (saves us time in the shower).

3. Hire a woman to pretend she is us and go to all school functions looking perfect.

4. Force our children to live in their playhouse.

5. Order take-out before anyone arrives home and pretend we just made it.

6. Change our name to Mrs. Roboto.

7. Invent edible toys. Merge dinner into play-time. Less clean-up.

8. Biodegradable clothes—it's the key to the future. You'll never have to wash again.

9. Marry a rich man.

10. Have your husband quit his job and stay home while you go to work outside the home. The house may not be clean but no one will care.


Finally, we aren't living in a perfect world; our economy isn't perfect or our environment. The weather is never perfect and neither is the justice system. So why do we expect our hair to be?

## Chapter 9

## The Trouble:
## We Expect Too Much From Men

"Why don't you understand?" we ask.

"I'm trying to understand. I almost understand."
Men say.

"You can't possibly."

"All right, I'm lost," they admit.

How many times have we had this conversation with our man? We try and explain women things to them and we expect them to understand. But they can't understand because if they could they would be a woman. Understand?

When we come out of these little agonies of womanhood, men will look us over nervously as if we just had an epileptic seizure and ask if we're all right.

The problem is we expect too much of men. They haven't been able to figure us out for generations, so why do we expect them to be able to now? How can we expect them to understand anything about our emotional reactions? You see, men are under the delusion that when there is a problem, you just solve it. However, women like to vent. We don't want to hear solutions to our problems. We want to play Shakespeare and lay down in distress and say "Woe is me." Unfortunately, if there is a man anywhere around while we are doing our woes, he is coming up with solutions. Regardless of what he says, we are going to say "Woe is me." If he would just wait a couple of hours for us to finish our "Woe is me" dissertation, then we would say his ideas were great. Unfortunately, men don't understand about the waiting period. I once told my husband that I didn't want to hear solutions, rather, I wanted to be upset—in fact I never wanted to hear solutions!

### Never expect men to remember little things

Men aren't used to having so many little things to remember that they have to buy a planner just to write under Tuesday, "Buy toilet paper." In fact, they remember things because we remind them. That's the reason men never write anything down, because they know we will write it down for them under "Buy toilet paper."

### Never expect men to get excited about updates

We also expect men to show their excitement

over good news in the same cheerleading fashion we do.

"Oh! Jack and Jane are getting married, isn't that wonderful!" we say, bouncing.

"Yeah, that's good."

"Yeah, but isn't it just so romantic how he proposed?"

"Yeah, nice."

"You don't seem very excited. What's wrong, don't you like her?" we ask.

"Yeah, she's fine."

"Fine! After all she's done for us? I would think you could be happy for her."

## We expect men to be calm and rational when relatives are visiting

This means calm enough to avoid scenes in front of the house guests. When our kids were little, we had a couch known as the "trial and error" couch, cheaply purchased—especially for those not yet potty trained. Once, when my mom was visiting, she insisted on sleeping on the couch. My husband insisted she take a bed. Finally, he convinced her with the words, "That couch has more urine in it than a public toddler pool!" After this scene, Mom, who doesn't want to be a bother (if she didn't want to be a bother she would have taken the bed when I suggested it) and a grandmother who feels her grandchildren can do no wrong, simply said, "Really, I hadn't noticed," and headed for the bed offered.

## We expect men to be able to fix everything

Some men are about as handy with a wrench as they are with a diaper. My dad was an excellent TV technician, yet, he was the kind of man that if your glasses broke he would take a big piece of duct tape and wind it around until they were "as good as new."

## We expect them to like whatever we cook

Women expect men to like what we cook. After all, we put love in it, right? It shouldn't matter that we zapped a four hour turkey for only 5 minutes in the microwave. Those waves are strong—they kill all bacteria.

## One thing we can expect

There is one thing we can expect from men that will never change: they will be totally bewildered by the female gender for the rest of history. They will spend eternity wondering what makes us tick and what causes all those emotional outbursts. They will wonder why we love roses and chocolate, but most of all why we put up with them.

## Chapter 10

## The Trouble:
## We Want Romance, Not Science Fiction

Women should never watch Romeo and Juliet because from then on, unless a man is willing to die for us, we won't date him. Everything he does compares with Romeo. We expect him to be at our window reciting us a poem; in reality, however, we have a hard enough time getting them to remember to open the door for us.

### Romeo's time

Men in Romeo's time just seemed to be naturally romantic. They didn't have to ask what we needed, they just knew. They always knew just what to say to win their lady's heart. It was something sweet complimenting her fair beauty.

Men don't recite romantic poems anymore. It's always the microwave way (the one-liners). Nowadays women get, "Hey, where have you been all my life?" As they think to themselves, "Avoiding you." In the olden days, if a woman let a man romance her, it was because he stood under her window in the rain for three nights serenading her. Now men think by saying, "Hey baby, did you happen to see the most beautiful girl..." that we are going to drop our lunch and say, "I'm yours." The humorous thing is that men are always complaining about being rejected, but don't have a clue why.

## We make it hard

I do have to admit when men are ready to get serious we are tough on them—especially when they propose. Everything has to be right: the right atmosphere, the right song playing on the radio, and the right time of day so we will remember it for the rest of our lives. This is a lot of pressure. I don't remember the first time my husband asked me to marry him because he asked me so many times before I finally said yes. I had to say yes—he was beginning to bug me. I'm weak that way. I knew I wasn't going to get rid of him, so why not marry him? After that punishment, he would think about leaving.

When he bought my ring and tried to put it on my finger, I had just had all four of my wisdom teeth pulled. I remember saying, as the anesthesia was wearing off, "Just put the ring on my finger before I throw up in your car." He has those words to cherish forever.

## What is this need within

What is it about the female species that needs romance? First of all, if you are good-looking you know it, right? Okay, so then if you know it, why do you need someone to tell you, unless you're vain. Second, we know when someone likes us—they are always hanging around. We know they need us. So what is really the point of all this romantic stuff? I'll tell you what. It creates the mood. The mood for what? Romance.

## Romantic dinners

I don't understand what is so romantic about candlelight dinners. You can't see the person sitting across from you and if we would rather not look at them maybe we shouldn't be dining with them. Dinner is for eating, not courting. After a candlelight dinner, all you can do is sit on the couch, thinking, "Dinner was delicious. I wish I could have seen what it was."

Once my husband took me out on our anniversary to a popular roadhouse. Although the food was excellent at this place, the atmosphere was anything but romantic. At this restaurant, every guy was wearing a sleeveless shirt and looked like Patrick Swayze. Loud country music blared in the restaurant and there were peanut shells all over the floor. Surveying the place, I thought, "If I had wanted to eat in a place with a floor like this I would have stayed at home and eaten in my own kitchen." As we sat over dinner, I eyed the peanut shells strewn across the floor and the tin roof and I said, "I bet this place compacts down into a dumpster at night."

### Romantic strolls

People speak of romantic strolls on moonlit beaches in Hawaii. But don't we spend more time taking pictures of the scenery than of each other and isn't the fact that you can afford to go to Hawaii romantic enough? I don't know about "The wind in your face and sand in your hair." Sounds like a ride I once had on the back of a three wheeler. Besides, after a long walk I'm ready to nap.

### Must-remember dates

We are very strict about men remembering all the important dates and details of every moment of our lives together. If they don't remember, well, they just don't love us. Our wedding anniversaries, for example: is this really something we want to remember? Especially since during most weddings there is some kind of tragic event such as the cake exploding or the best man showing up drunk. Now that leaves people talking. In fact they remember our anniversary better than our husbands do.

### Birthdays

We get really upset if our sweetie doesn't remember our birthday, and yet we won't allow him to discuss our age.

I guess when you are in love every holiday is a romantic one, or is supposed to be. This is confusing for men, who ask, "Why are you crying, honey?"

"Because it's Labor Day and you didn't remember," we reply.

"Remember what?" he says.

"That it's a holiday, so we're supposed to light candles and exchange gifts."

## The mood can change

One thing about women is that the mood can change so quickly from "Sleepless in Seattle" to "depressed in Detroit."

Then we will say, "Oh, the mood is gone."

The man confused will ask, "What? What mood? Where did it go? Maybe I can find it and bring it back." And they will go and hunt for it.

## The big deal

So what is the big deal about all this romance? Why do we women need it so much? I suppose it has something to do with knights on horses defending their ladies. Somehow barroom brawls just don't compare. I guess maybe we just want to make sure men are worthy of us. We figure if they try hard and make a complete fool of themselves they must love us. An assurance that they won't be off saying to the next pretty face, "Hey, where have you been all my life?"

## Chapter 11

## The Trouble:
## We Are the Most Likely Gender To "Buy A Bridge"

Whenever women make an important decision—you know, the decisons that affect any living organism other than us—we feel we must consider all aspects. Thinking, "If I do this it is going to affect my family, my banker, the lady who does my nails, what is the position of the moon that time of the month? Will it be raining?"

We are trying to avoid hurting anyone's feelings. It doesn't matter that we are making it difficult for ourselves with these deep searching questions such as, how will Sparky Junior feel when we change his dog food? How will it affect our Uncle Marky when he sees we've done this to Sparky? And what about Sparky's birth father, Sparky Sr. How will he feel? ( Sorry to bother the reader with southern problems. If you have a solution, please write me. )

## What other people think

Another problem we have is that we care too much about what other people think. We will ask a stranger if she likes our hair a certain way and if she says yes we have found our style! If we have ten people over for dinner and they eat all the food on our table except for one person, who barely touches the food, we go on a mission to try to figure out why.

We shower them with kindness and gifts. Then we find out this person suffers from an obsessive disorder and now wants to be our best friend. Now we have to think of a safe way to get rid of them that doesn't involve the police or them being medicated.

Men could care less about this nonsense. If they like Jimbo he is their friend for life if they don't they don't call him to go fishing. Not one feeling involved.

## Consequences

It would be easier for women to make decisions if we didn't have to worry about the consequences on the universe. The world is going to keep revolving whether we buy control-top pantyhose or regular. And we make it harder on ourselves by asking men what they think because, of course, we hate whatever they think. However, it does give us some incentive to pull in the opposite direction of whatever they suggest.

## Women are too gullible

Women are born with the tendency to trust people whose only goal in life is to sucker them out of all their money. Because of our motherly instincts, we don't want to believe that all the crime we see on TV happens anywhere outside of New York.

We want to believe that the preacher who ripped off 100,000 people had a mother who really needed an operation.

And that those "lose 180 pounds overnight" pills really do work—of course you wake up in the morning and your husband's missing. (The bottle says nothing about the pounds being yours.)

We just want to believe the good. So when an auto mechanic tells us our car needs a complete overhaul, we think, "Well, he is a certified auto mechanic. I'm sure he must have had to take some kind of 'Mechanic-critic Oath.'"

## Men must prove it

Men, on the other hand, don't believe anything. If you listen to them talk to each other they are saying, "Oh, I don't believe it. No, no, show me the scar." They won't believe it unless you can prove it. I think this stems from too many "I caught the big one!" fishing stories.

In fact the only people they can be suckered into believing are women. That's why we always see men on talk shows complaining, "She robbed me blind; she said she just wanted to use the phone, said she ran out of jet fuel for her Harley!" Maybe men figure women are too gullible to be that deceptive. They are forgetting that if you are gullible you learn quickly not to be. It is more likely that they get absorbed in a pretty face, thinking, "I'm not a gullible man. I know all the tricks, show me the scar—later!"

## The tendency

So, knowing women have this tendency to trust the most mischievous people on earth; and that mixed along with our indecisiveness would make us—a blonde. No, actually, I am a blonde, and I resent all those blonde jokes because there are just as many brunette women just as stupid as we are. Besides, if you're blonde and you do something stupid, people just laugh because they expect it. They say something like, "What color is your hair?" And we have to check.

If you're a brunette, however, you have to apologize for your behavior, "I'm sorry I squirted the mustard on your shirt—it will never happen again and I will have it cleaned for you." A lot of hard work for a hair color, if you ask me.

Once I had a roommate in college (a blonde) who fell out of her chair in the library and got her heel caught in the hem of her skirt. She couldn't get up off the floor so she went crawling around the library, trying to fix this disaster. Of course, we laughed and laughed, but I have to admit we weren't surprised.

Now, when another friend of mine (a brunette) went rushing up to a microphone in what she thought was an empty room to pretend she was an opera singer, then realized someone was sitting in the back, we had to claim she'd taken too much of her medication.

Well, whether blonde, brunette, or green-haired, we are all different—women with different intellects and personalities. Some are a little too gullible and think professional wrestling is a sport. Some are a little too indecisive and have to ask what socks to wear. But I suppose if we didn't have these tendencies then men wouldn't have any "Guess what my wife did?" stories.

**Chapter 12**

## The Trouble:
## Women Have Limits And We Won't Stop Until We Reach Them

Men are under the impression that we don't know when to stop. Especially when we're trying to make a point. Can you believe that! We have limits on everything, so surely we must know when to stop. We have limits on how much we will pay for a designer blouse (it's the same as the limit on our credit card). We have limits on how many calories we can take in and still have those six candy bars. We have limits on how much sleep we can get and not feel guilty. So, of course, we have limits on when we are supposed to stop; that limit is reached when we think a man finally sees reason. Which can take a good couple of hours. And the limit on being upset expires as soon as the man comes and apologizes.

## Silent treatment limits

There is also a limit on our silent treatments, which depends on the sincerity of the apology. If it is a half-hearted apology then it is two to four days. We are not heartless. You see, we can be technical like men.

## Regrets

If women don't follow these rules and obey these limits then we have regrets. We begin to realize we should have brought up certain points. Then, no matter how sincere the apology, we are going to hold grudges. Which will surface as unfinished business during the next argument.

## "Woman nag" theory

It seems that along with this "never knowing when to stop" theory, men also have a "women nag" theory. Men are mistaken here because what is perceived as nagging women see as helping. It seems this is how men get out of doing tasks they don't want to do by using that "nagging" word. Like they may consider it nagging when we remind them about fixing the kitchen sink. We said "remind"—we didn't order and salute. Yet if our four year old asks, "Daddy, will you tie my shoes?", Daddy doesn't say, "quit nagging!"

## House cleaning

Men say another thing we don't know when to stop at is house cleaning. They don't realize they and their posterity are a big reason we have to do so much of it. Besides, it is a commonly known fact that the more we clean, the more dirt we will find. Women have a sixth sense about cleaning: we can feel the dirt. Men have a sense about creating it. And if the man helps us then we have to reclean because he doesn't follow our instructions. By the time we are finally done, the kids are arriving home and thus the circle of a woman's life begins again.

## Can't stop advice giving

Men also say that women can't stop giving advice. But we give each other such good advice like, "I really think if you bleached the hair on your upper lip it wouldn't be noticeable at all."

Men say that when our friend tells us her troubles, we always have to tell them what to do about them. Of course we do. What are we supposed to say, "Too bad your husband dumped you, your children are missing and you have cancer—tough break?" I think not. We are supposed to say, "Sue him, take a vacation while your kids are missing, and have an expensive funeral."

## The equality thing

Another thing we don't know when to stop at is this whole equality thing. Do we really want to be equal to men when we are so obviously above? I mean, I don't want to have to risk my neck on the battlefield on the front line in some third world country. I've seen war movies; no way do I want to be stuck on some swampy island with wet feet, dodging bullets and eating dinner out of a can. No sir! not when I can be at home, feet propped up on the couch, watching TV and eating bon bons all day. My mother didn't raise a fool.

I am proud to admit I like being home with little people who like me and still love me when I send them to their room. I don't want to get up at five, eat a donut and rush out of the house. I don't want to have to wear a suit every day. Or take orders. I guess what I'm trying to say is I like staying home, raising children and being an unappreciated mother. It gives me hope that in the future my unappreciative children will themselves have unappreciative children and my seed will carry on into all the unappreciative generations to come.

## Don't know when to stop with imagination

My husband is always teasing me about how I let my imagination run away with me. I keep telling him, my imagination running away with me is why I married him. Maybe now would be a good time to let him know I'm a writer and that my imagination is supposed to be out of control.

Men say we can create a mountain out of a molehill at any given moment. I view this as a talent. We can start by worrying about a freckle on our arm that could possibly be a mole, that could possibly be skin cancer, that could possibly cause us to go through painful radiation treatments, thus losing all of our hair. Then, after we are completely bald, find out the mole was benign! Now we are left hairless with a mole the size of Africa on our arm! I guess maybe we can go just a tad overboard.

## Men can be thankful

There is one thing men can be thankful for: that we don't know when to stop loving them. We are always looking for the silver lining in the dark cloud. As we rationalize, "He robbed a bank and shot forty people but he makes such a good beef stew." Men should just think of our never knowing when to stop as...persistence.

## Chapter 13

# The Trouble:
# Driving

Men are always complaining about women drivers. But if women are such lousy drivers, why are car insurance rates higher for men? I'll tell you why in just one word. Scenery.

When men are driving, their eyes are not on the road, they are on whatever is along the side of the road. It doesn't matter if it is a cow pasture that they have driven by fifty times. They will still be looking to see what those exciting cows are up to next. And for some reason, the woman in the front seat clinging to the dashboard for dear life is no signal to them that their eyes should be on the road.

### Men's driving styles

Why do men always drive with one hand on the wheel and the other hand hanging out the window? Don't they remember hearing their mother yell, "Keep your hands in the car!" They must be dreaming that they are a stunt driver; and yet, lost in their dream, don't realize they are only going 25 MPH.

## Men are uninhibited

Men are totally uninhibited while driving. They can put on deodorant, change their clothes and, as they turn their stereo up to max, shave. They seem to think that the car is their own private little world that only those they desire to can peek into. They are in the space shuttle preparing to depart for the moon.

## Talk Radio

Men like to listen to talk radio so they can snicker all the way home about the person calling in, saying, "What an idiot!" while fifty people stuck behind him waiting for him to turn are saying the same thing.

## Horn Blowers

I love the line men give the police when they were involved in an accident, "I beeped the horn." Then when we come home and tell them that we almost had an accident they will ask us "Did you beep the horn?" and we will reply, "No, I was too busy swerving!" They will then look at us in disgust and ask, "Why didn't you beep the horn?"

## Gadgets and toys

Men also have to play with all the buttons on the dash. They feel like a toddler in a toy store as they adjust the temperature, the radio station, clean the front and back windshields, adjust the headrest and look in the glove box for a magazine to read in case the scenery gets boring. They have this need to adjust.

Women are the opposite; we figure on a clear day if we have to make it three miles down the road with the windshield wipers on high our husband will fix it for us when we get home. Then we won't have to touch it again until it rains.

## No mufflers

Men think that if a car without a muffler pulls up beside them it is an open challenge to race. It doesn't matter if they are driving a station wagon and the other car is a Ferrari. When they lose, they will just look straight ahead and act as if they were just trying to make the next light.

## Men and cars alike

Have you noticed that men look like their cars? I mean, you always see some guy that looks like he's lost in the 60s getting out of a multicolored microbus. A short little oval-shaped guy usually gets out of a Volkswagen, and a guy with chains around his neck and smoke coming out of his ears always gets out of a Camaro.

## Women's driving habits

I suppose I've picked on men enough but I simply can't find a thing wrong with women drivers—except that we get pregnant. Then the transformation occurs. The sweet little woman behind the wheel letting everyone pass now turns into Mario Andretti. Later, not only do our bellies become heavier when we are pregnant, but so do our feet and we find them sinking to the floor (but try explaining this to a police officer).

We also feel protective of our unborn child. We no longer sit by and let people cut us off. We are driving for two now. And we feel indestructible. We have hormones raging in our bodies that could fuel a jet. They seem to be ignited when we enter the car. We find ourselves yelling things out the window and speeding up to get around a tractor trailer. We figure we are already going 20 MPH over the speed limit—why would anyone need to pass? They don't like us, that's what it is!

We hear ourselves saying things to our kids like, "Everybody hang on, mommy's gonna put the pedal to the metal." My little girl once told me, "Red means stop, green means go and yellow means speed up, it's gonna turn red." I was pregnant at the time. I had to teach her the way the officers like it phrased. I told her that you should proceed with caution on a yellow light saying, "Look before you fly through an intersection, mainly for police officers."

## Taking down directions

One thing that women are good at is asking for directions; we always ask detailed questions. Like, "Does highway 53 connect by that cute little blue house on the corner?"

## Turn signals

Women love to use their turn signals. To check mail, or when pulling out of the garage onto our driveway. We love to see those lights flashing; it just gives us that Christmasy feeling all over.

## Mirrors

We are also thankful that men invented so many mirrors in our cars to check our hair and makeup. Especially the little one on the back of the sun visor to put on lipstick. Finally, a man designed something on a car that's useful.

## Not mechanically inclined

Unfortunately, most women don't know that much about cars. So when you tell us that the engine just fell out don't be surprised if we ask, "Can we at least make it home?" However, we do know the basics: "If I put gas in, it will run."

### Driving with children

Women, however, do have the skill of a tightrope walker when it comes to driving with children. We can hold a bottle, change a diaper, and seatbelt in six screaming kids all while we beat a train through the railroad crossing.

### Driving posture

My husband teases that I'm always hunched over the wheel with the seat scooted up on its highest level. I tell him this is just because women have shorter arms and legs, unlike men, who like their ancestors have longer and more flexible limbs.

### Perfect driver

Perhaps if men and women combined their driving skills we could make the perfect driver, but who wants to look at cows?

# Chapter 14

# The Trouble:
# Saving The World

As women, whenever our friend has a problem we are sure we can solve it. It doesn't matter what it is, there is a definite solution and we have it. Our friends are hesitant with our solutions because they usually involve some miracle cure using elephant dung.

When they are going through a divorce, we say intelligent things like,"Well, I am sure Mr. Right is just around the corner." Isn't that what they want to hear? Give them hope, will we?

## Real values

I feel the only way we are really going to make a difference in this world is by teaching our children. Yet the things we are stressing with them have nothing to do with real values.

1. "Don't chew with your mouth open."

2. "You can't wear that sweater; people will think

I'm a Democrat."

3. "Don't leave the toilet lid up; how many times do I have to tell you, this is a safety hazard. Do you know how many people have fallen in toilets and drowned?"

I think if we are going to save the world, we'd better start by saving ourselves. For example, environmentalists have been harping for years about all that hair spray we use. We could probably save the ozone layer if every woman from now on just wore lots of mousse. Simple enough. We might look a little greasy but our children would be able to breathe.

What about community service—instead of going golfing on Saturday we could just walk across a park and pick up litter. It's the same thing. Just a different object to retrieve.

Now, what to do about this mixed-up government of ours? Perhaps we could just pass a law that any politician who dated women younger than our teenager wouldn't be allowed to run. Of course then who would our candidates be?

Maybe we should just raise the age limit to 90 in order to run for president. Who wants to tell lies when they're that close to dying?

Perhaps we could help devise programs to pay off the national debt, like renting out all those rooms where George Washington slept.

When each First Lady redecorates the White House we could suggest she give the used furniture to the poor. I could sure use a new couch.

We could preserve the world longer if we all moved to one continent and destroyed all seven one at a time. When one is completely destroyed we could just move on to the next. And let's not dismiss the idea of condos on the moon. Maybe, instead of prison, if you commit a crime you're sent to the moon and given an AMC Gremlin to drive (craters in the streets are never fixed there either).

## People unafraid

Women really want to save the world because our children's future depends on it. We can't believe that the world is having such crazy problems. Like people suing each other over issues that involve cats eating grass out of someone's yard, claiming that the bare spot has traumatized them. However, half a million would take care of that. Doesn't it just want to make you slap the back of their heads and say, "Where is your mother? Didn't she teach you anything!" I guess the fact that there are people unafraid to go on national TV and admit they're a serial killer should tell us something. What are these people thinking, "I'm on a talk show—that FBI agent waiting at the door can't use anything I say against me." Talk shows are probably how America catches 90 percent of their criminals.

Well, if we're going to save the world, we need to work together. But no color schemes and fancy party decorations, okay? Just the important issues such as:

1. Why does makeup cost so much? Don't the manufacturers know we are trying to save them from a society of ugly women?

2. Why do grocery carts always have one wheel that goes opposite of the rest? Is this some kind of bag boy rebellion?

3. Why do bags of chips have more air than chips?

4. Why can't we take the tag off the mattress? You can pull the ones off your clothes. It's not like we are ripping off the washing instructions.

5. Why do pantyhose slide down when you walk? Is this man's idea of a gag?

6. Why do mouth washes taste like medicine? Could we just rinse with a bottle of Robitussin?

7. Finally, why don't they pass a law that all women, before giving birth, must be drugged out of their minds? Do you know that some hospitals don't even offer epidurals for delivering mothers? Okay, I don't want to terrorize you. I'll stop. I do know when.

I am going to get off my soapbox for a while to focus on some of the good things going on in the world. When I have the time to come across them. I don't want you to feel all the burden the last millennium of women did who had the job of saving the world.

## Chapter 15

## The Trouble:
## The Need For Drama

My friends lead soap opera lives. They don't intentionally; however, things just seem to happen to them that would only happen on a soap opera. But that's okay because when I complain to my husband about how boring my life is I can always say, "But I have friends who lead exciting lives!"

Although I'm the writer in the group, my friends have the ability to weave a plot. For instance, their teenager stayed out all night. They will suspect that he is secretly working for the CIA on a drug-related mission because they found some pot in his desk drawer with a suspicious note signed, "You know who to give this to." That could only mean one thing. CIA.

My husband once asked me, "Don't you have any normal friends?" and I replied, "Ah, normal is boring; I like excitement! With friends like mine, who needs cable?"

Women love to believe that there is something exciting going on somewhere in their lives (which they hate to call normal). Even if it means that the man painting their house is really a serial killer because they saw something that looked like red paint (but they're sure it's not) in a bag in the back of his paint truck.

## Done it, did it, doing it tomorrow

Have you seen the soda commercial where the kids are saying, "Done it. Did it. Doing it tomorrow"? That reminds me of some of my friends. There is always one who, no matter what you say, has experienced it herself and has a great story to tell. It's fun to make up something totally outrageous, just to see what they will say. "So I heard that a man wearing polka dot pj's robbed a liquor store today," we say. "Oh, I was robbed by him once except he was into stripped pj's then," they reply. I had a friend, once, who supposedly knew just about any movie star you could name. She always claimed she was going to be doing a movie with one. True? I don't know. But exciting!

**Chapter 16**

# The Trouble:
# Don't Realize The Need For Each Other

The trouble with women is that we don't realize how much we need each other. After all, if we didn't have each other, who would we complain to about men? I've tried the dog, and he's not very rational. Besides, if I needed to talk to someone while they slept, ate or dug holes in the yard, I'd talk to my husband.

Women are wonderful at sensing each other's feelings. We can call our friend crying and for some reason they will know we've had a bad day. Boy they are perceptive.

Women will also agree with each others' weird analysis. "You are exactly right, Helen. If more women potty trained their children later there would be less crime in America." Our husbands would say, "Potty training? This is new to me."

There are days when I tell myself I have a good man, children to raise—I don't have time for women friends. However, this idea is a farce, and I remind myself of that every time the toilet overflows. And I have a choice of calling a plumber or my best friend, Ann. Which line do you think would draw more sympathy?